i gave myself the world

catarine hancock

central
avenue
PUBLISHING

2023

This is a work of fiction. Names, characters, places and incidents either are the product of the author's imagination or are used fictitiously and any resemblance to actual persons, living or dead, business establishments, events or locales is entirely coincidental.

Published by Central Avenue Publishing, an imprint of Central Avenue Marketing Ltd.
www.centralavenuepublishing.com

I GAVE MYSELF THE WORLD

Trade Paperback: 978-1-77168-282-4
Epub: 978-1-77168-283-1

Published in Canada
Printed in United States of America

1. POETRY / Women Authors   2. POETRY / Love

1 3 5 7 9 10 8 6 4 2

for the teenage girls that were, are, and will be.
this world is yours for the taking.

trigger warning:

this book deals with topics of mental health, body
image, emotional abuse, and sex.

please take care.

author's note

i gave myself the world uses the major arcana from tarot as a narrative tool. you don't need to be familiar with the meaning of the cards to understand, relate to, or enjoy this collection. i chose the major arcana as my inspiration for this book because much like life, the path it follows is not linear. it is not simply point a to point b. rather, it is filled with ups and downs, moments of progress followed by moments of regression, healing from one thing and then being hurt by something else. it reflects the reality of how we go through life. it will never be a smooth uphill climb. there will be days spent tumbling down, days spent sitting at rock bottom. but you will always be, in some way, moving forward. if there is one thing you should know about tarot going into this book, let it be that: you must move forward, always.

you are standing in front of your mirror, studying yourself. the weight of desire drapes heavily across your shoulders. the desire for what, exactly, you are not yet sure of.

a voice from inside you, but not quite your own, asks, "what is it that you want?"

you dwell on the question, eyes flitting over your reflection. you look tired.

that voice repeats itself, louder this time: "what do you want?"

it dawns on you, ever so slowly, what your answer is. you want to be happy. you want to feel beautiful, like you belong in your own skin. you want to be free, unrestrained in your existence. you do not want a life rid of hardship; rather, you want the ability to handle it in a way that is less debilitating, that leaves room for growth. you want it all. you want everything.

after a moment, you answer:

"i want all this world can give me."

there is a pause, and then the voice responds:

"then you're going to have to give it to yourself."

the fool

today is a beginning.
it is the softest of awakenings:
the fluttering of an eyelid
as you turn towards the sun.

there is a world out there,
and you are reaching for it
with fingers spread
wide and wanting.

a hundred paths twist
across plains and oceans,
through forests and caves,
over valleys and mountains.

you don't know which one
to choose just yet.
they all call to you
with their own unique songs.

it's okay to not know
which path is yours.
what's important is that
you are taking the first step.

i looked in the mirror
and saw somebody beautiful
staring back at me
with wide, eager eyes,
lips curled in a smile
as if to say
finally.
finally,
you see me.

—*that fateful day*

oh, how i hungered
for a new beginning.

to move to a town
that didn't know me at all,
to tell it
this is who i am

and not hear
but that is not what
we think you are
in response.

—*on escaping your hometown*

i will never forget
my first night alone
in my new apartment.

how i fell asleep
smiling,
dreaming of all
the possible things
i could do the next day
because for the first time,
everything about my life
was truly and completely
my own.

—*limitless*

how many more excuses
are you going to give yourself
every morning when you wake up?
how many more doors will you close
before seeing what's on the other side?
how many chances at happiness will you miss
because you're too afraid to reach for them?

—*when is enough, enough?*

sometimes
what looks like
a single step
is really a plunging fall
into a world
you never expected
to become part of.

—*snowball*

one of the best choices i made
was to open my mind to the possibility
that maybe the thing
i least expected
was actually the best thing
to ever happen to me.

you showed me so much
of myself.
you introduced me to
pieces of me i never
thought existed,
and i am so grateful.

but there was always
one piece i could feel
hiding in my heart
that you tried to stay away from.
and i would reach for it,
but i could never quite
grasp it.

after a while,
i realized that
it was a part of me
i was meant to discover alone.

and maybe it was curiosity
or maybe it was desperation,
but i had to know.

i had to.

—*maybe one day you'll understand*

it is 8:27 a.m. on a tuesday. your alarm is set for 9, but you woke up
early. in the extra moments, you soak in the feeling of the day. it
feels different.

"today will be a good day," you say, trying to start things off on
the right foot. you taste the feeling of inevitability in the air, as
though something has shifted overnight and a wheel has been set
in motion. a small smile graces your face.

"yes. i think today will be a good day."

you dwell on the idea of a fresh start, unsure why it does not scare
you anymore. at 9, your alarm dings. you debate hitting snooze,
even though you're wide awake. for once, you decide to get out of
bed on time. it feels like a puzzle piece clicking into place. again,
you smile to yourself.

to new beginnings, you think, and head for the shower.

the magician

only you have the power
to create a universe
that is just how you have
always dreamed it to be.

this may seem to be
a daunting task,
but look at all the seeds
you have already planted.
look at the roots
already digging deep.

you are the artist
behind this masterpiece.

and oh,
the art
you have already
created.

for so many years
i gave my writing the face
of the last one to kiss me,
the smirk of whoever
broke my heart last.

and now,
i am happy and healed enough
to not want to give my poems
his blue eyes or brown hair.

rather,
i create them in my likeness,
with my chocolate eyes
and my dark curls,
my round cheeks
and laugh lines.

so now,
instead of seeing a ghost
when i look back at these pages,
i will just see

me.

—*lookalike*

i can't tell you
exactly when
i started to love myself,
but one day i woke up
and thought,
you know, i really do
deserve everything,
and since then,
that's just how
i've lived.

i don't apologize
for the way my body
moves anymore;
i don't hold it
to some unattainable
standard.

i don't stop myself
from exploring
new things,
i don't care
if they're weird
or uncool
or "not like me."

because i really do
deserve everything.
i deserve the life
i've dreamed of.

i spent a lot of time
trying to fit
into a mold

not meant for me
before i realized that
i am supposed to
create my own.

so this is your sign.
look into the mirror.
step away from the
ill-fitting mold
somebody else gave you,

and make your own.

—*you are your own artist*

i don't know where
i'm going just yet,
but at least
i'm going
somewhere.

beginning to believe
that you are enough
is one of the hardest
battles you will ever fight.
self-doubt will whisper
in your ear at every turn.
it will beg you not to
break the hold it has on you.
it will cling to you,
teeth and claws sunk
into your soul,
and you will have to tear
yourself free from its grasp.
it will hurt,
this escape. this liberation.
but it will be worth it.
in the end,
it will be worth it.

i spent so long
dreaming about what
i wanted to become,
rather than working
towards it.

i wasted years
where i could've been
experiencing life,
living as my uninhibited self,
and instead, i only lived
that life in my head.

there is nothing i regret
more than waiting so long
before finally gathering the courage
to make it a reality.

my dad always warned me
about spending too much time
looking down, and it wasn't
until i turned 22 that i figured out
what he meant, when i started
looking up and thinking,

now this, this is something
i want to remember.

so start making plans. create a pinterest board and title it "manifesting" or "what i'm working towards" or "who i'm becoming." fill it with mundane shit, but shit that you want anyway, like photos of outfits you'd like to wear or plants you want to fill your apartment with or books you want to read. fill it with photos of the countries you want to visit and the cities you want to live in, the streets you want to walk down and the parks you want to sit in. fill it with the career stuff, too, like the stages you want to perform on, the discoveries you want to make, the conferences you want to speak at, or the classrooms you want to teach in. fill it with the family you'd like to have, the way you'd like to decorate your wedding, the house of your dreams. pin everything you see that makes you think, *that would be nice to experience.* every. single. thing. because life is more than just your clothing or your bedroom décor or even your career. it's about everything. everything that brings you joy, that adds a piece, however small, onto the mosaic that is you. so don't be afraid to want a little bit of all the world has to offer. it's in your best interest to try and experience as much of it as you can.

you sit at the desk in your bedroom, staring at the blank page in front of you. you feel compelled to express your excitement about this sudden feeling of starting again, this newfound discovery, but can't find the words. you can feel them tumbling around inside of you, but can't figure out the right order to write them down in.

"perhaps i'm not meant to be able to express this yet," you say with a sigh, gnawing on your bottom lip in frustration.

you aren't even sure of what you'd write, anyway. *i am growing into myself, finally, after all this time*, perhaps, or *i am starting to paint my own picture of what i want my life to be*. but you're afraid that you may lose the magic these words seem to carry if you write them down or even say them out loud. so you set the pencil down and go about your day, content to bring these feelings to life in a different way.

the high priestess

there is a small voice
inside you
that grows day by day.

she whispers your name,
louder and stronger
each time.

she tells you,
"i can show you
all you want to know.
you only need to open
the doors for me."

you ask,
"what is it that you have
to show me?"

she says,
"only the simple truth.
there is only one way."

you ask,
"what is it?"

she answers,
"trust in yourself.
you have all the answers
you need within you."

whenever i think of all the times
i should have listened
to my intuition but didn't,
a part of me twists with sadness.

how much heartbreak could
i have been spared if i hadn't
ignored that churning feeling
in my stomach.

how many tears would
never have fallen if i had
done the hard thing and said no,
or walked away.

so i listen to my intuition now
for the girl who didn't.
whose scars i now bear.
whose grief i now carry.

one of the first things i learned about my mother is that she is almost always right:

her predictions about the friends i make or the people i date almost always come true, even if i don't want to believe them at first.

and sometimes when the ending she predicted arrives, i want to ask why she didn't do more to protect me. which is not to say that she doesn't protect me, because she would if things became dangerous, or excruciating. but there have been times when she knew her daughter better than her daughter knew herself— stubborn and always wanting to see the best in people who didn't deserve it. so she would say, *i don't think that girl is a good friend*, or *he will do it again, he does not deserve your forgiveness*, and i would argue back viciously, the way only mother and daughter can argue, until i'd come home crying one too many times. and she would hold me each time without fail, knowing that i was learning the lessons she could not teach me herself.

—*sometimes, mother does know best*

your body has seen more than you know and remembers more than you realize. it still knows the touch of a lover you haven't thought of in years. it would pick their voice out of a crowd in an instant. it holds memories your mind might have long forgotten: how you got that scar on your knee, how old you were when that freckle formed, the exact way their mouth tastes. your body knows more than you could ever understand, and sometimes, it realizes something faster than you want to accept. so while it's screaming at you that whatever you're about to do is a bad idea, and your mind is working overtime to explain why it's not, take a moment and think about all your body has been through and how much of its experience you can hardly recall. think about how much the body remembers. and trust it.

—*gut feeling*

a woman's intuition:

many will fear it,
and many will doubt it,
but you should do neither.

it is one of the greatest weapons
you have.

sometimes
i feel as if i'm watching
my life play out in front of me
like it's a movie,
and my intuition is a helpless audience member
watching everything collapse
around me, shouting,
watch out!
and the words
falling against the white sheet
of the screen.

she screams,
you cannot trust them,
you cannot stay!
and pounds her fists
on the armrests as i do—
blindly, hopefully—
and she wipes tears
from her eyes as
i grieve the betrayal
and the ending.

she pleads,
you know better than this,
you know this is not good for you,
and begs on her knees
as i question the obvious,
as i convince myself otherwise.
and when i learn my lesson,
she is there to congratulate me,
to tell me through the screen,

you're getting there, sweetheart.
you'll learn to listen to me eventually.

you'll know
when it's time
for you to go.
it will begin
as a small prick
in your stomach.
a tiny whisper
in the back
of your mind.

whether or not
you go is up to you.

but no matter
how long you deny it,
that sensation will
only grow,
until it is coursing
through your veins
and screaming in your head.

at some point,
you will have no choice
but to listen to it.

—*you can't ignore it forever*

it is always painful
when the person you assumed
would betray you ends up
proving you right,
but trust me on this:

it is far less painful
to be proven right
from a distance
than to be caught in
the blast at close range.

—*set your boundaries*

if you cannot trust yourself,
who else can you believe in?

only you can truly know
what it is your soul wants.

don't let somebody take
that certainty from you.

don't let somebody try
to tell you that they know

what it is you want.

sometime during the night, you awake to find moonlight streaming across your sheets, painting your room and skin in silver. you open your blinds and stare up at the night sky. you wonder about the stars and the moon. how peaceful it must feel to always know who you are. you wonder if the moon ever felt like she couldn't trust the tides, like she was afraid they would one day stop pushing and pulling as she willed them to. you think of your mother, who you used to think knew everything and then learned otherwise, how she flailed when you reached adulthood and danced out of her grasp, becoming your own person. you think of your ex, how they told you over and over again that you were crazy. that you didn't know what you were talking about. you think of the way you have doubted every choice you've made since you turned 13. since you fell in love. since you realized life did not exist in black and white.

when you were young, trusting your gut seemed easy. you chose the toy, the outfit, the game, with ease. nothing was complicated. or at least, nothing was so complicated that the choice became impossible. you ran when you felt afraid. you screamed when you were angry. you cried when you were sad. you laughed when you were happy. you didn't analyze how you felt; you simply reacted.

the moon glows, her light gentle compared to that of the sun. there is a steadfastness in her. she knows exactly who she is.

from your bedroom window, you watch her, and you yearn to have that kind of belief in yourself.

the empress

love flows from you
endlessly.
feel it as it streams
through your veins.

that warmth you hold
for those dear to you?
it is something special.
something beautiful.

do not fight it.

nurture it.

help it grow
into something
extraordinary,
and give it back
to yourself.

do you remember
the last time
you put yourself first?

i mean really, truly
put yourself first.

the last time
you made what you needed
a priority and didn't waste time
weighing the feelings of others.

when was it?
was it last week?
last month?
last year?

or can you not remember
the last time?
perhaps there hasn't even been
a first time.

you give so much, darling,
and ask for so little in return,
and in some ways,
that is beautiful.

being kind to others
is a gift many people
in this cruel world lack.

but maybe,
just this once,
be kind to yourself.

some days loving myself
feels like a battle
i'd rather not fight.

and i've learned that
it's okay to take a moment,
to rest when you need to,
and it's okay to be happy
with where you are,
even as you take the next step
up the mountain
you've been climbing
all these years.

some days loving myself
feels like a battle,
and i'm ready to charge
towards it headfirst.

but other days, loving myself
feels like putting the sword down
and reaching for peace instead.

other days,
loving myself
feels like taking a moment
to appreciate how far i've already come,
and just enjoying the view.

i've started telling myself
i am beautiful
at all hours of the day.

when i first wake up,
all messy hair and morning breath,

when i get out of the shower,
skin reddened by hot water,
hair plastered wet to my scalp,

when i get dressed for the day
and i examine myself in the mirror,
i say it.

i say it before and after
every meal,
regardless of the number
on the scale.
even if i hate the way
clothes fit me that day.

because it is always true.

so i say it.
and i believe it.
every time.

affirmations to tell yourself each morning:

1. i am of the earth. i am a child of moss and morning dew. i am grounded; i am rooted in the depths of who i am.
2. i am strong. i have braced myself against life's highest waves and powerful winds and have come out on the other side, standing tall.
3. i am beautiful. i am ethereal, radiant with beauty. i have a smile as bright as the sun, and eyes that sparkle with the light of a thousand stars.
4. i am loved. i mean so much to so many people. they would not be the same without me in their lives. their skies would be darker without me.
5. i will overcome. i have faced much adversity and i have conquered it all. i am ready for the next obstacle, the next challenge, and i will defeat it, just as i have all the others.

you have sealed away
your love for yourself.

perhaps
it is time
to finally

u n l o c k

the door.

—*let it all in*

i got my love of books from my mother. my desire to eat home-cooked meals over fast food. my affinity for fancy clothing and pretty gowns. i learned how to dress by watching her in the mornings. my first barbie came from her childhood collection. she taught me how to have pride in myself, and the satisfaction that comes from looking put-together. she helped me learn how to stand up for myself. when i wasn't happy at school in 4th grade, she didn't stop until she knew why, and then she put my happiness over everything. she taught me how to swear, how to turn my words into weapons if i needed to. she made sure i always knew i would be loved, no matter who it was i fell in love with. she let me figure some things out on my own because she knew i wouldn't listen to her no matter how hard she tried. some of those things were outfits i wore, or the way i filled in my eyebrows, but some of them were the second chances i gave, or the friends i made. we talk every single day. sometimes i call her because i'm bored, and we talk for two hours. when i come home, i follow her around like a lost puppy. sometimes at night, she will come lie next to me on my bed and demand i tell her a story about my life now. she is the only person who i know, without fail, will always think i am beautiful. she instilled in me my love of words, and now i am a writer. in many ways, this book is just as much hers as it is mine.

—*mother*

i came into womanhood
fists swinging, screaming,
you will not make me small.
i went to war and i won,
but it would be a lie
if i said that i did not
pay a price for it.

when you are a teenage girl,
you earn side-eyes and sneers,
snide remarks muttered when
they think you can't hear them.
everything you love is a joke
or foolish or unimportant,
and everything you hate is just
too smart for you to understand,
too sophisticated, something only
men might be able to grasp.

so i came out on the other side
larger than life, and god did i smile,
scream *fuck you, you did not keep me
from being myself* at the world.
but a piece of me broke during
those years, cracked under the pressure
of being mocked for liking
boy bands and romance books,
taylor swift and love poetry,
converse and bulky sweaters.

i think every young person
experiences a second youth
in their 20s where they rediscover
all the things that brought them joy

when they were younger, and i don't
think anybody experiences that more
than those of us who were teenage girls.
we spend the better part of a decade
being condescended to because of . . .
well, because of everything,
and our every move, interest, and idea
is belittled and picked apart by boys
and men and even our own mothers,
who usually don't know any better.

so we get to be 20, 21, 22,
and suddenly we own stuffed animals again,
and start dressing the way we want to,
not for anybody else, and we
blast taylor swift and harry styles
and read smutty romance novels,
and it's like we are finding ourselves
all over again, because in many ways,
we are.

we had this piece of us—
the joyful piece, the curious piece,
yes, the childish piece—
completely destroyed.
and we spent the better part of 19 thinking
we did not deserve to get it back.

when i came out on the other side,
i smiled. i laughed. i even grieved.
and then i put on taylor swift
and rememorized her discography.
and when people scoff at me now,
i tell them to go fuck themselves.

—*the recovery of the teenage girl*

when my mother and i fight,
it is like screaming at a mirror.
i do not know which of us
hates that more.

—*one and the same*

sometimes i say things
the same way my mother says them,
down to the way my eyebrows move,
and my best friend laughs at me and says
you sound just like your mom right now,
do you know that?

when it first started happening,
it was scary, perhaps even insulting,
because i'd spent so much of my teenage years
trying to become different from her.
i'd seen the worst of her by then,
because what else are the ages of 12 to 18
but a parade of all the flaws your loved ones carry,
particularly all the flaws they tried to hide
or you didn't notice when you were younger.
i'd started to pick up on her anger,
the things that made her bitter,
the parts of her i pinpointed and thought to myself,
that is something i would like to not do.
she will not give me that.

but of course,
we all turn into our parents eventually,
and now i am adorned in her fingerprints:
my facial expressions, my sense of humor,
the speed at which i cry for reasons good and bad,
all of which i see as good things
now that i am not a teenager and not so angry.

and i suppose, despite my best efforts,
that i picked up some of her that i wish i hadn't,
that i know she wishes i hadn't either,
because she has told me

how much she hates those parts of her too.
at the end of it, though,
one day, she will not be waiting to pick up the phone
when i call randomly at 3 p.m. on a saturday.

and then,
i will be glad to have her inflections
woven indistinguishably into my speech,
her gestures so naturally incorporated into my own.
i will be relieved to have the comfort of looking into
a mirror and seeing her staring back at me.
i will say something the same way she would,
and i will think,

thank god.
thank god.

you are studying yourself in the mirror. every inch falls victim to your critiques. you pinch your thighs and mutter bitterly, "too squishy." poking at your stomach next, you add, "too big."

on and on this goes until you have called every part of you ugly or fat or wrong, from the hair on your head to the calloused heels of your feet. and at one point, maybe this would have made you feel better in some twisted way. maybe it would have motivated you to make some kind of change. but change that is rooted in self-hatred is rarely the kind that sticks or satisfies. how many times have you found yourself back here, still unhappy after months of cutting carbs or doing sit-ups.

once, you thought it would be enough to have a body like the ones you see in magazines. but you are realizing now, finally, painfully, that it is better to believe that your body is enough as it is, even if you want to make it stronger or healthier; that giving your body a goal to meet before you love it means you will always, always be waiting, loveless and empty, as you keep pushing the goalposts again and again.

you whisper to yourself, ashamed, "i don't know why i am so cruel to you."

your reflection simply stares back. it doesn't know either.

the emperor

don't be afraid
to dream big.

reach for the stars.

if you do not have
a leader in whose footsteps
you can follow,
forge your own path.

become that leader
for anyone else
who may need one.

i got my love of fantasy from my father. my nostalgic affinity for classic rock. my taste for fancy ice cream sundaes, turnip greens, and cucumbers and onions. he handed me my first toy sword and my first action figure. he helped me learn how to ride a bike, and over a decade later he taught me how to drive a car. he would come carry me home when i'd fall and skin my knees. when i started taking piano lessons, he would sit at the bench and help me practice. he was the first one of my parents to cry when i won my first voice competition. when i come home now, he still comes into my room to kiss my forehead before he goes to bed. every so often, he sends me a photo of one of our cats. we talk about the weather, not in a small-talk, *we-have-nothing-else-to-talk-about* way, but in an *i-raised-you-to-care-about-the-weather-and-now-it's-something-that-bonds-us* way. i call him when my toilet breaks or the check engine light comes on in my car. he is trying to teach me how to do taxes. i am trying to get him to read brandon sanderson. i got my love for it from him.

—*father*

i have grown
so tired
of feeling small,
of having my ambitions
looked down on
and my dreams mocked.

every condescending
wow, you've got big plans,
every empty
i'm sure you can do it
pierces my soul
like a knife.

i vowed to show them all
how wrong they were about me,
and i did.

i achieved everything
i said i would, and more.

and perhaps there were times
when i leaned a little
too willingly into
my spite as a motivator.

but i won't lie and say that
it doesn't feel good
when you accomplish something
they didn't believe you could,
and you get to say

look at what i've done,
and fuck you.

i am the perfect example of
do as i say, not as i do—

i tell them to eat more,
to get in their three meals
each day, but i am lucky
if i even eat one.
it's not purposeful as much
as it is a lack of time or caring,
which may be worse,
depending on how you
think about it.

i tell them they are beautiful,
to quit pinching stomach fat,
but then i do the same,
molding my soft thighs in my hands
and wishing for something different.

some days i am as hateful towards myself
as i have ever been, but i will not hear it
from them, will not hear a single
i shouldn't eat today or
i hate how my body looks.
i will tell them how beautiful they are
with a conviction i am rarely able to give
myself, and sometimes they will point
that out to me; they will say
why is it that you cannot give this love
to yourself?

and i laugh and shake my head, say
do as i say, not as i do
to avoid admitting that i don't have an answer
to give them.

i'm tired of writing about the same shitty guys,
the same ones who hurt me and made me cry all the time,
because they're gone now; they've been gone for a while
and at this point, i'm just adding more poems to this pile
of repeat metaphors and lines and the same old shit
i've been saying for years, and i'm getting so sick
of finding myself writing the same damn lines
about pain and healing now that i'm finally fine,
so i'm done writing about the same shitty guys.
i'm done giving them my art and giving them my time.
it took four books and about eight years,
but i've finally grown weary of writing through tears,
so this one is for me and for me alone,
about my dreams and my joys and what i call home,
it's about my soul, my body, my mind, my heart;
it's the book where i finally take back my art,
and it's about you all too and the way you will grow
as you get closer to loving yourself and just letting go
of the fears that you have or the grudges you carry—
i know that it's hard and i know that it's scary
but it's worth it in the end, i know for a fact,
and loving myself this way made me realize that
i'm done writing about the same shitty guys
who took up so fucking much of my sweet, precious time,
and the fact that i let them is almost a crime
because at the end of the day my poetry has always been

mine.

i took back everything
they'd taken from me
over the years
i'd wasted giving love
to everybody
but myself.

i stole back
my drive,
my patience,
my kindness,
my joy.

it never belonged
to any of them
in the first place.

—*reclaiming*

you're pacing in your room. the urge to do something, anything, is coursing through your veins. for the first time in a long time, you feel burning ambition, something you thought you'd lost. your old passions no longer lit a spark in you, and you walked through life half-awake, as though nothing could bring you to be fully present.

now, though, you are brimming with the desire to create. you'd almost forgotten what it felt like. but you want to make something meaningful. you want it to have an impact, however small. you want it to mean something. *you* want to mean something. and you can't remember the last time you believed yourself worthy of that kind of dream.

so you turn, invigorated, and grab your journal. you flip it open and reach for your pen. you stare at the blank page before you.

you start to write.

the hierophant

you are surrounded
by those who can guide you.

they may be friends
or family members,
with their tough advice
and kind reassurances.

sometimes they come
to you as a lover,
even if the lesson
they teach you isn't pretty.

but other times,
the world is your guide.

and when it calls to you,
listen.

if you take anything away from this book, let it be this:

it is okay to ask for help. it is okay to need help. you are not meant to do this alone. life is hard. it's hard even when you are surrounded by people who love and support you. to try and conquer it on your own is terrifying. you should not have to feel that fear. so please, reach out when you need to. someone will be there to answer. it may not be the person you expect or hope for, but they'll be there regardless. and you'll understand why it was them that came to you, one day. it will become clear, and you'll be so, so thankful.

reach out your hand.

let them take it.

i owe
everything
i am
to teachers.

this includes my parents and my grandparents,
all of whom were, or are, teachers.

but there are so many others:

my middle school choir director, who put me in front of a
microphone, told me to sing, and forever altered my life;
my high school choir director, who may have been one of the first
people outside of my family to truly believe in me;
my undergraduate voice teacher, who looked after me like i was
her own daughter and taught me to sing for joy.

those are just a few,
because every teacher i've had
has made some kind of impact on me.

and while so much of what i do is for myself
and the life i want to live, the person i want to be,
every victory, every milestone, every birthday
is also for them.

for the heart they so permanently changed.
for the memories i am forever grateful to have.

these are the kinds of people you should surround yourself with:

those who make you smile
those who make you laugh
those who know when you're shutting down
those who understand when you need space
those who don't make you feel small
those who celebrate your victories, however tiny
those who don't project their insecurities onto you
those who treat you as an equal
those who believe in you
those who will hold you as you cry
those who will call you on your bullshit
those who want you to call them on theirs
those who grow alongside you
those who are kind to strangers
those who hope for better things
those who are gentle
those who are loving
those who are good
those who are good
those who are good

don't you know?

we all have so much
beautiful growing
left to do.

i wish i could pull
the sadness out of you

unravel it like a string
from where it's wrapped
tight around your heart

i wish i could burn
the darkness away

light a flame in your chest
that won't go out
even on the days when your soul
is fraught with storms

i wish i could pull
the sadness out of you
but it's not up to me

i am not meant to be your hero
i am not meant to be your savior

i am meant to be your friend

i am meant to hold your hand
when the thunder inside is too loud

i am meant to hug you close
when the string tugs too tightly

i am meant
to listen
to understand
to love

i wish i could pull
the sadness out of you
and i will tell you that every day

but that is not
what i'm meant
to do

—*but i'll always be here for you anyway*

you're walking down a street in your neighborhood with your best friend. you haven't been the most responsive lately, but you finally accepted their invitation to get coffee today, and you're glad for it. you've missed them. life has become chaotic and busy, filled with too many obligations, leaving too little time for anything else.

"how are you?" they ask, and a million answers fly through your brain:

i feel as though i'm being pulled in a hundred different directions. i'm trying to figure out who i am, but i don't even know where to start. i am so scared. i am tired of growing older, tired of discovering new difficult parts of life. i can't catch up. i'm drowning. god, i'm drowning.

and pulsing underneath every sentence that drifts around your head is: *i am alone. i feel so alone right now, and i don't know what to do. please tell me you feel this too. please tell me you know what i'm going through, that you share these burdens. these fears.*

to them, you say, "i'm fine."

but because they are your best friend, because they know you better than anyone else, they don't believe you for a second. they look you in the eyes. say your name.

"what's really going on?" they press.

so you take a deep breath.

and you tell them.

it's the lightest you've felt in months.

the lovers

on darker days, remind yourself:
where is love if not everywhere?

it lies in your best friend's laugh lines,
in your partner's tender touch.

in the sound of music being made,
in sunlight filtering through the trees.

in the compliments people give to strangers,
in small, random acts of kindness.

my dear, love is in everything,
and in you.

always
in you.

in the past,
i always thought of a lover
as a necessity,
as important to have
as air or water.

now,
i think of a lover
as a desire,
something i could live without
but wouldn't like to.

in the future,
i hope to think of a lover
not as a necessity
or a desire,
but as an embellishment:
the cherry on top
of an already wonderfully
complete life.

—*shifting perspective*

i love
with arms wide
open—

heart bared
for my lover's hands
to wrap around.

i love
the way i need
to be loved—

with honesty,
with understanding,
with joy,
with everything,
everything,
everything.

i have fallen in love
with the way
i love people.

i've grown to know
that they really are lucky
to be loved by me,
in the same way i am lucky
to have our hearts
so closely intertwined.

there is so much more
to love than romance.

my best friends have outlasted
every one of my lovers.

i fear losing one of them
more than a breakup.

the end of a romantic relationship,
i know how to handle.

but the thought of the end
of a platonic one?

it is scarier than
any lover ever leaving me.

—*platonic soul mates*

when they touch your thigh for the first time:

yes, they find you hot. sexy. delicious. a body they could worship at the feet of. a mouth they want to dip their fingers into. a neck they could run their tongue along. but do they find you interesting? smart? equal? do they ask before they touch you? do they *see* you? do they say *tell me more*? *show me that song you like. i like to listen to you talk, i think you have such wonderful things to say.* do they tell you *i love how you see the world*? do they find you beautiful in the way you laugh, do they become mesmerized by the way you admire the changing of the seasons? do you feel desired for more than just your body? it may have been the hardest lesson for me to learn, but the most valuable: to know how to see one's true intentions. to figure out how not to place love where only lust is waiting.

i've started telling people i love them more.
it's become a typical way to end a conversation:

i'll talk to you tomorrow, love you.
i'll see you tonight, i love you.

these words used to feel so sacred to me.
i felt afraid to tell them to anyone.
but now i say them daily,
to more people than i can count:

my grandmother, at the end of a phone call,
my best friends, wrapping up a voice memo,
drunk in a bar bathroom, laughing to tears,
waiting to go onstage, holding hands in the wings—

i love you.
you mean so much to me.
i love you.
thank you for being there.
i love you.
i'm so glad we're experiencing this together.
i love you.
get home safe.

MY LOVE LANGUAGE MUST BE:
after zane frederick

honesty / nervous hands / those *i think my soul already knew you*s /
the moment before we kiss for the first time / you saying *i love you*
into my mouth / when we know each other so well we don't have
to speak / comfortable silence / how it seems hard to everyone else
/ but we make it easy / never doubting / *i made the right choice
in loving you* / so i stay / and you stay / and it's just the way we
dreamed it would be

let me tell you how you deserve to be loved. you deserve to have somebody who sees you at your worst and does not shy away. you deserve to be with somebody who holds you up on the days where you can barely stand, who guides you towards the light when all you see around you is darkness. you deserve somebody who wants you even when you don't want yourself. you deserve to be loved in a way that is kind and forgiving. that does not make you feel bad for being angry or sad or sleep-deprived or busy. that does not ask you to put your dreams aside. but if you want that, if you want that kind of love—and you want it to stay—you have to be willing to give it, too. if you do not want to love somebody that much, that completely, you will not find it waiting for you. at least, not for long. you see, the ones who can love you in the best way are the ones who have faced heartbreak and pain and have come out stronger because of it. they have every reason to shut themselves away and fear the worst in a relationship, but they don't do that. they know that they deserve to be loved the way they love others, and one day, they'll find it. so they keep trying. they love and love and sometimes it works and sometimes it doesn't. they know when to run, when they've given all they can but have had nothing given to them in return. but they will love you for all time if you can meet them halfway. if you are willing to give them what they give you. this is how you deserve to be loved. by good people with good hearts. by the ones who know what love really takes.

you are pondering romantic love.

you've held it and lost it many times in your life. you've basked in its warm, soft glow and yearned for its return when the cold of loneliness sets in. somewhere along the way, though, you stopped . . . needing it. hungering for it.

and it's strange, really, the way the desire for romantic love faded without you noticing. you replaced it with more reliable things. you found a soul mate in your best friend. a life worth living without someone sharing your bed. a home you feel comfortable in by yourself.

of course, you still want it, someday. you still hope to find it again, and that this time, it will stick around. but you don't *need* it anymore to be happy and content. which, you suppose, will make its return into your life that much more beautiful; it will arrive when you are not looking for it.

you think back to when you were young and so afraid to face life without a lover, so sure that they were the ones to make you worth something. but you realize now that you are worth everything on your own. your value will never be determined by the ones who leave you. and it will never be determined by the ones who stay, either.

you are still everything when you are alone.

the chariot

you know
exactly
what you want.

you can feel it
bubbling,
pulsing,
twisting
inside of you.

but where there once
was only desire,
there is also now
willpower and determination.

you want it,
so you will have it.

you dream it,
so you will live it.

i remember exactly how it felt, the first time i believed in myself.
i don't remember how old i was or even what was going on, but i
remember the feeling. at first, it felt foreign to me. but it was an
adrenaline rush like no other i'd experienced. it was that feeling
of rightness, that sensation i spent much of my teenage years
struggling to find and hold on to. the constant ringing of *i know
i know i know* deep inside me. i don't know if i was 3 or 7 or 12.
maybe it was right before my first piano recital. maybe it was
as i stepped onto the soccer field. i could've gone out there and
botched every second afterward, played every note wrong, missed
every goal, but i don't remember that. i just remember that for a
moment, nobody could have told me i was not meant to be exactly
where i was. i knew, beyond a doubt, that i was right where i
belonged.

god, but when did i lose it?

i had had it once,
so when did it slip
through my fingers?

was it the first C on a math test
or the grade school bullies who
didn't let me go a day unscathed?

was it my first heartbreak
or the friends that laughed at me
more than with me?

perhaps it was all those moments,
and all other moments like them,
that took it from me, little by little.

so quietly and subtly
that i didn't even notice
until one day, when i reached for it,

it was gone.

i got it back
piece by piece.

i pulled it from
the jaws of trauma,
wrenched it from
the grasp of toxicity.

i fought for it
tooth and nail.

and slowly but surely,
over many years,
i rebuilt it.

and now that i have it back,
now that i once more feel that
almost-forgotten beat of
i know i know i know—

i am
never
letting anybody
take it from me
again.

my belief in myself is an anchor.
it is steadfast and infallible—
an unbreakable constant.

it keeps me from floating
too far out to sea,
from allowing the waves
of self-doubt to pull me down
and drown me.

you can't wait for
a grand sign to take
your next steps.

at some point
you must simply

become.

there is another rejection in your inbox.

you barely read past the first line—"thank you for your application, but unfortunately . . ."—before exiting out of your email and walking away.

they say that life is 99% rejections and that all you need is that 1% to make it. just one yes to launch your career. just one yes to make your dreams come true. just one yes to change your life. and that's true, in theory, but it doesn't make the nos hurt any less. it still stings every time somebody tells you they aren't interested in what you have to offer.

and you know you have something great to give if somebody were to just say yes. but with every no, that certainty you have about yourself wavers. each *unfortunately, we are unable to offer you this position* and *please consider reapplying next year* adds another weight threatening to pull you under. and sometimes, it feels like it would be too easy to simply never put yourself out there, never take the risk, again.

but you refuse to quit, even as the image of that email burns in your mind. you refuse to let it take you down.

"one yes," you tell yourself, "all it takes is one yes."

and you are going to get it.

strength

oh, broken one,
the things you have seen.

you have survived
the many trials
life has thrown in your path.

how you have bled
and wept and ached—
but oh,
how you have fought
and healed and lived, too.

you have such bravery
in your heart.

more than you know.
more than you will
ever understand.

think of how many times
you wanted to quit
but didn't.
how proud you were
when you made it through
to the other side.

you always have that strength
inside of you.

even on the days
where you cannot find it.

especially
on those days.

they pushed you into the water
when they knew you couldn't swim

hoped you'd reach for their hand
hoped you'd make them your savior

but instead
you kicked and fought
against the waves

instead
you taught yourself
how to survive

because you knew
you didn't need
somebody like them

you knew
the only person
who could save you

was yourself

we have spent lifetimes
trying to make ourselves smaller
trying to quell a flame
not meant to fade to an ember

it has taken us years
to realize that being born
with fire is not a curse
but a blessing
and that we are not
something meant
to be tamed

together
our burning
will destroy the bars
meant to cage us in

our flames
will scorch through the ropes
meant to tie us down

we are just beginning
and we will not let anyone
put us
out

—*change is our destiny*

to every young person out there who is afraid:

this world will only get better
if we fight for it.

we know what is right.
we know what we must do.

our futures depend on *us*.

it may sometimes seem to be
an impossible task.

but know this:

we are
so much stronger
than we realize.

—*together, we are unstoppable*

life is one long
battle of resilience.
we are always recovering
from something while
preparing for whatever's next.

you compare
women to flowers
as if that makes us weak,

something to choose from
and throw away,
something fragile and temporary.

as if we do not survive
your coldest winters
and harshest summers,

as if we are not more
than what you
think
we are,

as if we don't
grow back
no matter
how many times

you knock
us
down.

you may
have knocked
me over

punched the breath
from my lungs

but i will never stay
on the ground
i will feel the air
again

and i will rise.

it was a rough day.

you barely left your bed. you hardly ate anything. you cried. you cried until your stomach hurt and your throat burned and your nose was so clogged you couldn't breathe out of it.

but days—or weeks, or months—like this are nothing to be ashamed of. you are learning this, slowly. it takes a lot to embrace the darker parts of yourself, the parts that aren't so shiny and pretty. the parts that need to cry, need to lie in bed all day. the parts that need to be alone sometimes.

you can't ignore them. so the best thing you can do is let them know that you see them and you will give them what they need: an hour to cry. a day to rest. a week to heal.

but at the end of it, you have to get up and keep going. you have to let those parts of you know they are not in charge. you must feel them, experience them, and then keep going. one step at a time.

for that, you know now, is strength: to see the darker parts of your heart, to feel them full force, and to do what you need to do to keep moving forward.

so now, at the end of this terrible, terrible day, you get up and wash your face. you throw out the tissues and drink some water. you order from your favorite restaurant for dinner and put on your comfort show. and when tomorrow comes, you will keep going.

the hermit

there is a peace
that settles when
you sit alone
with your thoughts.

an understanding of
your soul emerges,
but only if you are
not afraid to embrace
the scarier parts of you.

all you must do
is take some time
for yourself
and gather the strength
to look inward.

how many more pieces
of myself am i willing to lose,
to bury deep within me,
to swallow down
just to please
somebody else?

when will i learn
that that isn't love?

i always hoped he'd become a better person, that he'd change and grow, and one day i'd be able to look at him and say, "look, we were 16, everybody does shitty things when they're 16," but every time his name comes up in conversation, it's accompanied by the latest terrible thing he's done. for a while, i thought maybe i was the wake-up call, the final nail in the coffin of the person he used to be, but it doesn't seem that way. it hurts to know i was just another pit stop, another place he rested for a while and set fire to before moving on to whoever grew to love him next.

but there's nothing i can do about it now. i've done my time and found my closure and healed my wounds and at some point, he won't have anybody left to burn through. and thankfully, that simply isn't my fucking problem anymore. some people just don't want to change, and it's never been my job to try and do it for them. maybe i learned that a few years too late, but i'm glad i learned it eventually. even if it cost me.

and it cost me.

is there anything scarier
than the realization
that you aren't sure
of who you are anymore?

i look at my reflection
and see a nightmare staring
back at me.

and if i cannot recognize myself,
who else will?

i know
i have much more
to give—

this heart holds
cities,
stars,
entire galaxies—

i just wish
i could find
somebody
worth giving
it to.

i am either too much for somebody or not enough,

but never just right.

on the third day of october,
it rained: a soft, light drizzle
dancing across the pavement.

i cracked open my living room window,
let the breeze carry in the scent
of wet leaves and the changing season,
listened to its gentle song.

i thought, at least
in this time of confusion
and not being sure of much else,
i still have the rain.

i find comfort
in loneliness.

there is no greater time spent
than the time you spend
getting to know yourself.

you are lying alone in your bed. it is late, 2:13 a.m. to be exact. it is quiet, except for your head. your head is never quiet.
you say to nobody in particular, "i don't think i like myself."

there is a moment of silence as if you are waiting for a response. of course, nothing comes, and you didn't expect anything to.

"i am afraid that i am turning into a version of myself that nobody, including me, will like," you say softly. "it wouldn't matter if nobody else liked me, as long as *i* liked me. but i don't even like me. i am too . . ."

after a brief silence, you finish your sentence. your voice is barely audible as though you are confessing a great sin, which, in some way, perhaps you are:

"something. i am just something."

you are not sure what it means, but at the same time, you understand precisely. afraid to say more, you roll over, pull the covers tight up under your chin. at 2:58 a.m., you drift into a fitful sleep, pondering the meaning of "something"—if it means too little or too much or not much of anything at all—and what it means that you feel so strongly acquainted with the sensation.

the wheel

they say
fate works in
mysterious ways.

it can be kind.
it can be cruel.
it can be boring—
so boring that you
may be stuck wondering
whether fate is paying
you any mind at all.

but don't be mistaken;
fate is always working.

don't ever think
the wheel is not turning.

it is in motion
from the moment
you are born.

i wonder about the doors
that closed throughout
my life,
the different paths
i walked away from.

i wonder if there's a life
out there where
i still dance,
a life where i fought
against the awkwardness
my body seemed predestined
to carry until i could
leap, twirl, and plié
with as much grace
as the rest of the girls in my class.

i wonder if there's a life
out there where
i still play piano
the way i did
before i found singing,
a life where opera
never ignited
that never-ending flame
in me, and piano
remained enough,
remained all i needed.

i wonder if there's a life
out there where
i don't write,
a life where i never
discovered poetry,

never grew to need
to create it like
i need to breathe,
and i found other places
to bury my pain.

in all these lives,
i believe i am happy.
these versions of myself
do not know what path
they missed out on.
they've all found their own
passions and callings.

and perhaps
part of them longs anyway,
when watching an opera
from the orchestra pit
or going to support
their friend at an open mic,
just as i do when i see
a ballerina pirouette with ease
or hear one of chopin's nocturnes.

perhaps each of us is lucky
in our own different ways,
both blessed and cursed by
the lives we have created for ourselves.

and god, there are times when i wish i could be 16 again. before i had to make real choices. before i had to decide what career i wanted and whether or not that was even a good idea. before i knew what hating myself felt like. before him. before my idea of heartbreak changed from *he liked her more* to *he said he loved me but he lied and cheated and now it is all so confusing*. before things stopped being so simple. before i realized that a lot of the people i thought were my friends were actually unkind. there are times when i wish i could turn back the clock, go back to thinking the worst was over and not lying in wait ahead of me. but maybe at 27 i'll wish i could be 22 again. maybe this is the new best part of my life, the one i'll yearn for in 5 years. but at 16 i thought i was on top of the world. and at 22 i don't feel much like that at all. maybe that's wisdom. maybe that's growing up. or maybe it's the realization that adulthood is less romantic than you think it's going to be. i know that it's better too. i'm glad i have choices. i'm glad i am in control. i'm glad to know the difference between real love and cruelty. i'm glad i have true friends. but god, i wish i didn't have to pay for it. i think that's it—i don't really wish i were 16 again, i just wish i could have all this without the parts where i had to pay for it.

sometime after
we stopped talking,
you changed your profile picture
for the first time since i'd known you.

such a small thing,
but it gave me pause.

how strange,
i thought,
how strange to see evidence
of you changing and continuing on
without me being there to witness it.

perhaps there's a timeline
where it was enough
to have each other.

imagining that
makes it a bit easier
when i think about how
it wasn't enough
in this one.

where do we go
from here?

do we step back
and watch each other
from afar,
hoping that
if we are meant
to forget,
we'll each be the first one
who does?

can we still let
each other know
we care?

would it be a crime
to let you tell me
you miss me?
would it be a crime
for me to say it back?

in the end,
does the rope holding us together
fray and snap?

in the end,
do we stop
trying to tie
ourselves
together?

THREE TRUTHS:

1.

not every door is meant to stay open. sometimes all it is going to
give you is the power to close it. so close it.

2.

some people will not love you. either they won't know how or
won't want to. but others will fill their shoes. there will always be
people who love you. don't worry.

3.

take a deep breath. some things just need time. maybe a little,
maybe a lot. but not forever. i promise, you will not wait forever.

if you're the one
waiting for me
at the end of this,
i'll run to you
with open arms.

but if it's
somebody else,
or nobody at all,
i'll run towards
the end anyway.

and i'd like to think
that if we never speak again,
one day you'll look back on me fondly
as somebody who didn't fear the future
when they pictured you by their side.

i'd like to think
you'll remember me
as somebody who loved you
the best they could,
even if it wasn't always what
you wanted or needed.

i'd like to think
you'll remember me
as somebody you could
have spent your life with,
if only the timing had been right.
if only we'd worked for it
just a little bit
harder.

it's interesting to see where the pieces fall, how they end up connecting, often in ways you never saw coming.

you are thinking about this now as you stir your morning coffee. all the things that happened to bring you here, standing in your little kitchen. you wonder how it could be different. who might you be if you'd said yes instead of no that one time, or the other way around? who could you have become if you'd stayed with them, or never been with them in the first place? who would you have loved otherwise, if at all? what hobbies would you have picked up, what books would you have read, where would you have gone?

you take a sip, letting the flavor wash over your tongue. it's no good thinking about it now, of course. the decisions have been made already, perhaps long before you were born, if you believe in things like destiny or fate.

it's a curious thing to consider, isn't it? how maybe there was a path already mapped out for you, and you've blindly been following it your whole life. in some instances, that's just about the worst thing in the world to think about. it's almost nauseating how horrifying it is.

but in other instances, like today, as you drink your coffee, it is a sweet, gentle comfort to believe that somehow, all will turn out as it should, and that you are exactly where you need to be.

justice

i know that
anger burns in you,
but you cannot
let it consume you.

trust that those
who have wronged you
will pay the price
for their cruelty.

justice
always finds its way
to the ones
who deserve it.

you knew who i was from the beginning.
i told you i would always put myself first,
and i never once faltered,
and you loved that about me, didn't you?
loved how i wasn't needy,
loved how i could make my own decisions,
loved how i was headstrong and determined
and unafraid to go after what i wanted.

but now you hate me for it.
now, i am cruel to value my own future so highly.
now, i am selfish to do what i need to in order
to be happy and achieve my dreams.

your love was always conditional,
you spat at me when it was over.

and yours was not?

—*hypocrisy*

the rage in me is a tempest.
it slams itself against my rib cage,
strains against my skull.
some mornings i wake up
and i am so angry
i can feel it radiating
underneath my skin,
gathering in the tips of my fingers.

one time he left me
in the middle of the night
because i wouldn't have sex
with him, and i forgave him
because that's what you do
when you've loved somebody
for that long.

three days after we broke up
for the first time, he tried to fuck
one of my friends, and i forgave him
because that's what you do
when you are trying to fix a mess
you had a part in making.

he told me when we broke up
for real that his friends
thought i was a crazy feminist,
and i didn't forgive him for that
but i did laugh. i did smile
and shake it off because even though
i was free, i was still in love with him
and that's what you do.

you forgive, or ignore, or try to understand,

and you tuck the anger away.
and the storm brews until eventually
you're far enough away from the shelter
you built to protect yourself from hard truths
that you can finally feel the rain.

the rage in me is a tempest,
and i forgive him for it because
i gave him a storm too.
and maybe it's bigger than mine
but for all the wrong reasons.
maybe he won't ever forgive me.

and maybe there's a small part of me
that's afraid of being left at 4 a.m.
because she said she was too tired.

when she rears her head,
it is a downpour.

don't spend your time
with those who
tread on you.

you
are nobody's
doormat.

you don't exist
for others
to wipe their feet upon.

—*you are worth more*

there's nothing
quite like a woman's rage:

the anger that comes
with being grabbed
and tossed around
against our will,
the fury that accompanies
condescending smiles
and unapologetic interruptions.

it's an anger
that sits for years.
it simmers quietly
until one day,
it begins to boil
right over the top
of our patience.

so go on—

take our rights,
and see our anger.
hold us down,
and face our fury.
touch us again
and b r e a k
under the wrath
we have held in
for centuries.

and if you're not afraid?

well,
you should be.

stop waiting for them
to apologize for hurting you.

you will waste time
you should be spending
healing and growing,
on words that will often
be empty or underwhelming.

just know that,
in one way or another,
they will be sorry.

when they see you happy,
glowing without them there
to dim your light,
they will be sorry.

when they realize
they were just a lesson
you conquered,
they will be sorry.

—*don't bother waiting for closure*

you don't have
to forgive them,
and you certainly
don't have to forget.
do those things only
if they feel like
the right choice for you,
not the result
of somebody forcing your hand.

i realized neither
was the right choice
for me.

i found peace and healing
much quicker when i stopped
trying to make myself
forgive and forget.

so i remember everything.

and i forgive none of it.

you're learning to be okay with being angry.

there are a lot of reasons for it these days: all you have to do is open up twitter or turn on the news.

but that's a comfortable anger for you. it's easy to be angry at those things. it makes sense to be. in fact, it angers you even more when you see people not getting angry about them.

but it is hard for you to be angry at the ones you love. even if they deserve it. maybe especially then. forgiveness seems so much simpler, but it doesn't leave you feeling any better in the long run.

so you are learning to be okay with being angry. with speaking up for yourself and being honest about how you feel. and the people who really care about you do better or, at the very least, try.

but the people who don't care about you make no effort, and each time you ask them to, they make you feel small and foolish.

a year ago, you would have apologized, said you were just being dramatic. but now? now you know better, and you give them exactly what they deserve from you.

not a single fucking thing.

the hanged man

the best things
in life take

time.

they must take root
before they can
sprout;
they must be nurtured
before they can
blossom.

do not rush
what is not yet
ready.

you will be grateful
you gave it the time
it needed when at last
it stands before you
in all its beautiful

glory.

i have spent so long
wanting to escape the cycle
of lopsided dependency,
to be free of lovers
who make me the glue
that holds the pieces of their lives
together.

i am weary of relationships
that turn into cages.

i long for a love that frees me.

if i'd known
it was our last conversation,
i would've asked
you more questions.
i would've listened
more closely.

maybe i would've
seen the writing on the wall
and said,
it's okay.
i can feel this distance too.
i don't know why
we thought it would be easy
to keep each other close.

what if my happiness
isn't as relatable or entertaining
to read about as my sadness

what if people
stop wanting to know
what i have to say
about the life
i'm living, now that
i'm happy it's mine

—*nothing new*

i hope i don't haunt you,
hovering over your shoulder
like a cruel phantom,
reminding you at every turn
of the life we once dreamed about,
the one i let go.

i hope you are living in peace,
free of me and my unreasonable
expectations and hypocrisy,
and i hope one day
you find it in you to forgive me,
if only because that anger
is going to eat you alive
(trust me, i would know).

you'll be better off
without me, i swear.

let that be the one promise
i don't break.

i was angry for a long time at so many things
i've long lost count of them all.

and there is no point in listing them here anyway,
for you can find them all in my writing, somewhere.
but the one thing i never wrote much about,
not until now, was that the person i am angriest at
is not him, or those who didn't say anything.
it is myself. i am angry with myself,
though i don't deserve it.
i have put down the anger that i have held towards him
but have yet to put down the rage i feel towards myself,
about what, exactly, i am not even sure of.

i am angry, maybe, for being angry? i am mad that i sat so long
at the right hand of fury. that i allowed him to take up
so much of me, long after he should have stopped mattering.
that his fingerprints smudge so much of my art.

now that i have no fire left in me to burn him with,
i am scorching my own skin with its remaining embers.
and how cruel is that, to know that this anger has no place
here anymore but to still let it take its time on its way out,
to let it leave brand-new scars atop the ones i had finally
finished healing.

i have always had a knack for falling in love,
not with people as they exist in front of me,
but with my idea of them and what they could become.
and every time, it ends the same way:

i am disappointed, drained of energy
from trying to make somebody into a person
they simply are not, having allowed myself to morph
from girlfriend to mother to therapist and back again,
and they hate me for it, often rightfully so,
because they did not expect such changes
from me, because they feel my love was not true.

and that is what hurts the most, i think,
because i loved them deeply, so much so
that i believed they were capable of greatness,
and is that not love? to push people to become
the best versions of themselves? to experience
growth alongside each other?

but the truth is, that kind of love has its limits,
and often, i don't know that i've pushed too far
until it is too late, until i am faced with the realization
that i was trying to make somebody who was already
a good person, a kind person, into someone who
fit better with me, rather than accepting that
we were simply not meant to be together.
and i am left with yet another person who
resents me for trying to change them so
i could stand the thought of marrying them.
another reckoning for myself because, once again,
i have been naive in love and selfish in my interests,
and i have once again hurt a person who did not deserve it.

my friends make jokes about how i am a fixer,
how i leave my exes in better shape than i found them,
but i don't know if that's really what i do.
because while i leave them with sharper clothes
or a stronger sense of ambition, i also leave them with
the sense that who they are at their core is not enough,
and that was never the case, it was just that who they
are is not the right person for me. and that is not
a bad thing i should put effort into trying to change
as much as it is a sad thing i should accept, grieve,
and move on from, so i do not leave behind
somebody who may now know how to cook
but has a horribly warped sense of self.

the next time love comes along—and i will wait for it—
i want it to be somebody i can look at and accept,
completely, for who they are in that very moment,
not the person i think they could be in a year, or five, or ten.
i want it to be somebody with whom growth feels easy and equal,
who fits into my life like a puzzle piece. i want it to be somebody
i can make sense with. i want it to be somebody who,
when we're holding hands in public, doesn't make people scratch
their heads but rather causes them to say,
"yeah, those two? those two belong together."

you're tired of settling.

you've spent your whole life doing it: relationships, jobs, plans—all the times you felt yourself nestling down into something that fit nicely in your comfort zone but never pushed the boundaries. never fulfilled you the way you really desire.

but you're tired of it, now. so you're aiming for something bigger. a love that doesn't feel so hard to maintain and tight on your skin. a job that acknowledges your worth. and plans that are big and ambitious, because you're capable of following them through.

it's scary, to allow yourself to want something more. but you know you deserve it. you know you'll be happier for it. more than anything, you know it takes time, and it's in that time you'll find yourself wanting to fall back into old habits.

but you're tired of settling, so you buckle down and you wait.

as long as it takes.

death

life is filled
with endings—
moves, graduations,
breakups, retirements.

and don't these all lead
to new places and people,
new chances and memories?

for what is an ending, really,
if not a brand-new
beginning?

i like to think that
we all die several times
over the course of our lives
before we die in the
physical, funereal, buried
kind of way.

personally,
i have watched
myself die time and time again.

the ballerina me died at 9
when i told my mom i wanted to quit.
the athletic me died at 12
when i walked off the soccer field
for the last time.
the naive, romantic me died at 16
at the hands of someone who
should have known better.

and i grieve, some days.
i mourn the lost versions
of myself because they
were beautiful,
and a lot of them deserved better.
and while some of those deaths
were through no fault of mine,
many of them were.
most of them, in fact.

i cast them off to crumble to dust
with a simple choice,
a mindless decision.
and i don't regret it,

even as i allow myself
to feel sad about it.

because if one of those
versions had lived,
if i had made the choices
that would have kept it alive,
then the me i am now
would not exist.

the countless variations
of myself fading away
with every yes or no,
every left or right,
were worth it to get here.

to get to the best version
i can be.

i don't know who i am if i am not grieving something, which is to say i don't know who i am now that i am no longer grieving him. for so long, i have been mourning the death of us, long past the end of the funeral. each year, i'd find a new way to dig up his grave until one day i found there was nothing left to unearth. where there once was a corpse, there were flowers blooming in its place. what once was a grave was now a garden. and i think that represents how i grew after him, how i became something beautiful in the aftermath of something so ugly. some days i still don't recognize myself without his shadow in my eyes, but i am learning to. some days i miss having a gravestone to visit, but i am learning that having a garden is so much better.

—*stormy gray*

i never told you this,
but i'm not sorry i left.
i'm just sorry that i had to.

so time goes on
and i fall in love
with somebody new,
and maybe you fall in love
with somebody new too,
but either way,
you delete our photos,
and i don't ask you to meet
up for coffee, because
you don't want
to see me anymore,
and i broke the promise
i made to you, i know,
but i couldn't have predicted
the person i'd become once
we broke up any more than
you could have, and we swore
to always be friends, but
look at us now:

more distant, more like strangers
than we were before we even met.

the thing is that i still love you, but i'm not *in* love with you anymore. and that feels weird to say. it feels bitter on my tongue, but it's true. when i kissed you last, it felt like you were home, but now i'm not sure we'd even fit into each other's sides the way we used to. your voice pops up in old videos and it still washes over me the way it always did, but it doesn't leave me feeling clean. i don't know what exactly it means to love you—because of course i do, you were so important to me—but to no longer want to be with you. i don't know how to navigate this new territory of *you still mean the world to me but you're not my entire galaxy*. in all honesty, i think i always knew we'd grow in different directions. i don't think you understand how much that would've hurt, to watch that happen. but i could already feel the growing pains, and they hurt enough for me to know i didn't want to wait around to feel the agony of the distance. so i love you, i do, you were my best friend, but you aren't my reason for breathing. i mean, to be fair, you never were. i don't love anybody like that anymore, but my day is okay, good even, without you being part of it. i mean, i hope you can forgive me for this, because i don't think you have. i mean, i hope that maybe one day you'll understand me, because i don't know if you did, in the end. i mean, i hope you're happy, or at least at some point you get there.

i was scared i'd never write again after my last book. it took everything, and i mean *everything*, out of me. and that's because so much of my writing was steeped in the pain i'd experienced, and i finally put it down. i finally walked away from it without any desire to come back, and i felt . . . empty. empty of words. for the first time in years, i had no poems left in me to write.

so i sat and waited for them to come. i searched that dark place inside me and found nothing waiting for me there anymore. and fuck, that was terrifying, to reach into the part of me that had fed me so many poems for the last six years, and come back empty-handed. there was a part of me that, against my better judgment, thought, *was the healing worth it? was finally being able to move past what happened worth this?*

and of course it was. i wouldn't have ripped that wound open again, not for anything in the world. but it was hard to look elsewhere for inspiration because for the longest time, i'd never had to. why would i? that gaping hole inside me was *pouring* out words. i never even wrote them all down. some slipped through the cracks between my fingers as i tried to catch them and press them to the page. there was a voice in me that wanted to hunt for those lost words. to find them and make something pretty out of them.

i was disgusted with myself. had i become so attached to my trauma that i was incapable of being an artist without it? i started writing about it to process it; the end goal was always to leave it behind. where did i lose that? i told myself, over and over again, that i hadn't, but i had. somewhere along the way, i got so very, very lost. so lost that the thought of writing something not about him, the idea of writing about things that make me happy or, god forbid, myself, was alien to me.

for six months, i barely wrote a word. it didn't feel right, to push it before i felt ready. *it'll come back*, i told myself. *it has to*. so i waited, and waited, and waited . . . and then one day, i wrote a poem about spring. and not as a metaphor for healing or moving on from a cruel winter-that-is-not-winter-but-actually-my-ex, but just spring. and then i started looking around at all the poetry surrounding me, and looking within at the poetry i had always carried inside. and suddenly, it clicked, and the poems were there once more, as fast-flowing as they'd always been, but more vibrant. full of life and joy and gratitude and peace.

i've always written for myself, and in those years, that didn't change. it was all for me, even if i had developed tunnel vision by the end of it. i'd needed to do it.

but once it was over, i needed to remember that my poetry did not begin with him.

and it never would have ended with him, either.

—*the rebirth of my poetry*

i don't think the 17-year-old version of me
would recognize the person i've become,
and i think that would make her very, very

happy.

today, you find yourself scrolling through your instagram feed, going all the way back to your very first post.

as you start at the bottom and make your way up, you swipe through cringeworthy selfies and old partners, the flame they sparked in you long since forgotten. you look back at nights spent with friends you no longer talk to, either because of time and growing older or because they ended up not really being your friends.

but the main thing you notice is how the light in your eyes slowly died as time went on. how at one point, they were practically screaming for help in every photo. for a few months, there was hardly a spark of joy in any post. you remember when some of those photos were taken, and you don't remember feeling so sad. certainly not sad enough to make you look like that. at least, that's what you thought.

as you keep scrolling, getting closer to the present, the light comes back. your smile seems brighter, the candid laughter caught more genuine. the sparkle returns. and it's reassuring to know that even though you still have so much growing left to do, and that you are still not at your happiest or best, you have already come so far.

so much of the life in you has already been reborn.

temperance

seek balance
in all that you do.

your life should be
an equal flow of
give and take.

you should never
be giving the best
of yourself only to
receive crumbs
in return.

put down the anger
you feel for your naiveté,
for believing somebody
who only spoke lies.

it may be the hardest thing
you'll ever do,
but you have to
forgive yourself.

you didn't know.
you couldn't have.

forgive yourself
for being vulnerable,
and for embracing the chance
to fall in love.

i suppose this is some form of grief: the feeling of emptiness after
finally putting something—someone—down.

but my art will still be beautiful.
its freedom from you will make it shine.

so i said
tell me about
the parts of you
that are cracked
and messy

tell me about
the pieces of you
you've lost
and can no longer find

tell me about
how they broke you
and how you had
to piece yourself
back together

i want to understand
how you have become
the person you are

i want to know
the reason behind
your barbed wire fences
and towering stone walls

trust me
i will not be scared
i will not run from you

i have known pain
just as you have and
i am not scared
of your wounds

so tell me
all of it

i promise
i will hold your hand
and listen

—*i can be patient*

there is a sense of equilibrium in my life now that used to be
absent. i feel at peace with the way things have fallen into place.
i give only to people who give back to me. i am rewarded for my
work. i feel appreciated. i feel respected. i feel good about where i
am and what i'm doing. for the first time in a long time, i feel like
i'm traveling down the right path, and i am aware of the direction
i'm headed.

i come back to my hometown
three months after i move away.
everything is the same,
except my father sanded and re-stained
the coffee table, and the living room couch
has gone off to get reupholstered.

but my childhood bedroom looks the same
as it did when i left, albeit cleaner.
there are still books left on the shelves
with dog-eared pages, waiting for me
to pick them back up, never knowing
that i left at all, that i forgot i ever started them.

my cats still recognize my face, something
you don't worry about until you move
three hours away and only come home on breaks.
they still meow and purr and curl up
into my side at night. my mother still
comes in and lies next to me in bed
and asks me to tell her some things.
so i say, i'm the happiest i've ever been,
i finally feel like everything in my life
is working out. i say, mom, i think i'm
in love. i think i may have found the person
i'm supposed to spend my life with,
but it's too soon to tell and maybe i'm just crazy.
i say, i finally feel like i'm my own person, like
i'm really starting to figure out who i am.
and she smiles, of course she does, and in her mind
i'm sure she's patting herself on the back for a job well done.

i walk around my undergraduate campus
and i notice how the leaves are changing,

in their shades of orange and red and yellow.
i don't remember paying them any attention
in years prior, but this time i take a photo.

my brother asks me why;
i simply say i've stopped walking
with my head down and started living.

—*when it all lines up*

recently, you've felt so much calmer than you usually are. everything used to make you nervous—would you be enough? were you asking for too much? were your expectations too high? were you rushing things?

but now, calm wraps around you like a warm blanket. the anxious thoughts you've been so well acquainted with for years are quiet.

it's strange, this gentle equilibrium you've found for yourself, but you are comforted by it. you don't know what choices you made to bring you here, but you're grateful you made them all the same.

the peaceful silence that comes with certainty is one of the best gifts you've received in a long time.

the devil

there are people
you will encounter
out there in this world
who will drain you.

it could be over the course
of five minutes or five years,
but they will leech the joy
from your heart.

and some of them
will be wrapped up
and topped with pretty little bows,
dainty lips over sinister grins,
gentle, soft hands with
fingers crossed behind their backs,
and you will want to trust them.
you will want to believe
they are good for you.

but you will feel the light
inside you dimming
ever so slowly,
and you cannot ignore that.

no matter the high
their attention may give you,
i promise you it is not worth
the low you experience
when you lose yourself.

don't let anybody fool you into thinking that putting yourself first when you need to is wrong. if the person you love acts as if choosing yourself is a crime, as if following your dreams is a slight against them, as if you cannot be your own person, understand what that means. it is not love; it is control. they don't love you. they love the way it feels to have you trapped under their thumb.

SOMETHING TO THINK ABOUT:

how much time
have you wasted
trying to make
other people happy?

how much of your life
has been spent
giving the love
you should be giving
to yourself,
to those who don't
deserve it?

i had to leave because it was
i could spend my whole life with you—
after you change,
and not
i would marry you right now,
as you are, and not want you
to be any different,

and it was never fair.
it was never fair.

sometimes
the hardest part about
letting go isn't
the act of loosening your grip,
but wondering what you'll do
with your now-empty hands.

i don't think anything hurt more
than realizing the parts of me
that pull people in,
that make them want me,
are often the same parts
they hate the most
by the time it's over.

you're so ambitious
becomes
you're so selfish,

you're not afraid to stand up
for what you believe in
becomes
it's annoying how political
you are,

you're so strong and resilient
becomes
you're a cold-hearted bitch.

and it never fails
to end that way.

i just want it to fail,
if only once.

how many times have i lost myself in love? how many times have
i let a lover grip me by the throat, replace my tongue with thorns?
i have drowned in love, flooded my lungs with its promises. and
each time, i find myself a shell by its end. i feel as though i hardly
know who i am if i'm not in love with somebody. it is the thing
i crave most from life. i am addicted to it, and i don't care how
painful the comedown is. it'll all be something worth writing
about, won't it? and isn't that a fucked-up way to view love? but it
is how i've come to see it. i want to be free of that. i want to know
a life without the constant strain of romantic love, without the
chokehold it has on me. give me six months free of it. give me six
months to turn that love inward and unleash it upon myself. let the
next person to come along know me not as the starved soul i have
become. let me know what it feels like to love a person for who
they are, and not for what they can give me.

you have to stop
mistaking toxicity
and unnecessary drama
for passion.

love isn't always
going to be easy,
but that doesn't mean
it'll be so hard
you forget yourself
completely.

they aren't your soul mate.
they aren't the one.
this isn't going to make
a good story, just a sad one.
there is no happy ending
with them.
the only happy ending you'll get
is when you walk away.

you know deep down
this isn't how
you deserve to be treated,
and you also know that
this isn't what good love is.

stop lying to yourself.
go. just go.
you won't regret it.

i promise.

somebody comments
under a post of mine:

i miss when you wrote sad poems.
can you do that again?

and i think:

why would you miss me
hating myself?

—i'm a real person behind these words

it's a saturday night, and you're staring at yourself in the mirror again.

it's been a while since you've done this—picking yourself apart for things you cannot control. you're frustrated with yourself for tumbling back down to this point when you'd been doing so well. but it can't all be a straight uphill climb.

it was what your friend—who really isn't your friend—said to you earlier: that snide comment about your outfit, the way their eyebrows raised as they looked you over. it was enough to put you back here.

they're not my friend, you think as you study yourself, still wearing that outfit they'd shit on, the one you were *so* proud of earlier when you picked it out.

"i think it's cute," you'd said to them, trying to defend yourself. "i feel good in it."

and when they'd only hummed in response, still wearing that *oh, you poor soul* expression, you felt yourself falling down, down, down again.

"i feel good in this," you say to yourself now. "fuck them."

how many times have you let them bring you down? how many years have you tolerated it? the thought of putting up with it any longer sickens you.

and so you decide, right then, looking at yourself in your outfit you like, to not put up with it a second longer.

the tower

sometimes life moves
in unexpected directions.
sometimes it's good,
and sometimes it can seem
as if just about
everything is ruined.

when it does,
you will stand there
watching helplessly
as it crumbles.

and when it all
comes crashing down
around you,

what can you do
other than wait
for the dust to settle,
and see what is needed
for you to rebuild?

the day we ended,
i felt my life irreversibly

shift.

what once made
so much sense
no longer did.

my view
of the world
was flipped upside-down.

for what am i

without you?

who am i

if not yours?

what is love

if not your name?

here's the thing:

it was going to hurt no matter what. it was going to hurt even though i knew it was the right thing to do. it was going to hurt even though the idea of staying cut me far deeper. i could not have avoided that pain.

but i still tried. i tried hard to tie us off with a neat little bow, to patch us up with flowered band-aids as if i hadn't just severed the relationship that had been my right hand for the last four years. i wanted so badly for it to be easy. because i loved you—and i love you still, in the way you love the ones you wouldn't have left if you'd only been different people—and you deserved to be left as gently as possible. i wanted you to understand that it wasn't your fault. i have spent my life loving and leaving. perhaps that is my curse. my way.

the anger came eventually, though, as it always does, and i could not pretend to hate you for trying to forget me. i could not even try to blame you for it. but this is what i will leave you with:

we were real. we were real and in love and it was beautiful. and now it's done. and i don't feel bad about it. i had to go, okay? i had to. i doubt i'll ever know if you forgive me for it, but i imagine one day i will hear of your happiness and that will be enough, for me.

it has to be.

so grieve them,
and grieve the piece of you
they took when they left.

cry until you have no more tears,
scream until you lose your voice,
rationalize, un-rationalize, then rationalize it again
until your brain can't form any more thoughts.

but in the end,
don't forget to dry your eyes,
drink your water,
and actually listen to your best friend
when they tell you it will get better.

because it will.
slowly at first,
but then one day,
you'll be surrounded by the life
you've built without them by your side,
and you will be proud of yourself
for coming so far.

listen to me:

you are still beautiful
even though they are gone.

you are still worthy of love
even though they don't see it.

you are still everything
you have always been and

you are strong enough to live without them.
you are strong enough to live without them.
you are strong enough to live without them.

say it until you believe it.

—*a healing exercise*

this is the worst thing that has happened to you. i know. i know it is. but it won't be the last experience you ever have. there will be so many more moments in your life that you'll want to see, i promise. the rest of your life won't be perfect. some of it will be bad. some of it may even be worse than this. but some of it—a lot of it—will be so, so good. and you'll be glad you stayed. this is not what defines you. this is not the sum of who you are. this is one small piece. don't let it take up more room than it deserves. don't let it be the last thing you know.

i didn't know
how badly
i wanted somebody
to look at me that way
until you did.

like you saw right
into the center of me,
like you knew my soul
from the very first second.

—*you were the last thing i ever saw coming*

you never thought this would happen to you, and it is killing you.

the agony is slicing through you like a knife. you didn't know it was possible to feel this much pain. sometimes, you're hardly able to breathe around the size of it. it's filled your body. you are made of what has hurt you.

it burns that you didn't see this coming. you didn't get a chance to steel yourself for it at all. it doesn't help that you are constantly thinking about what you could've done to avoid it, or what was left unsaid. those words haunt you more than anything else.

but you aren't without people to lean on, at least. your best friend is at your side, wiping away your tears and holding you tight. you have your family. they remind you of all you were before and all you will be again.

you think of how farmers burn what remains of their old crops after the year's harvest, how the flames clear the way for something new, how the ashes fertilize the soil so that the next harvest is even stronger than the last.

perhaps this was your fire.

the star

in this time of rejuvenation,
take a moment to be proud
of yourself.

you made it
to the other side.

despite what you believed,
it was not the end of you,
and the courage that got
you through is not yet
gone.

use it
to carry you
towards joy.

healing is long and messy and often unkind. it can leave you feeling lost and alone as you unpack the boxes of pain and sorrow. but one day, this house will feel like a home. the painful memories will be replaced with happy ones, and you'll never regret taking that first step towards the door.

when you are ready
to seek out love again,
remember this:

you shouldn't be trying
to replace what you lost.

you should be trying to grow
something entirely new
instead.

i knew from the start
this would be the softest
love i would ever have,

the most tender thing
i'd ever hold
in my hands.

i should have known
i was heading down the wrong path
when sitting down to write
felt like readying myself
for war.

i would think:

how many more times
will i turn myself into a battlefield
for this?

how many more times
will i marvel at the destruction
i make of myself in the name
of my art?

it's so gentle now—
the words spring from me
like a bubbling creek,
all peaceful harmony and flow.

—*a new kind of inspiration*

this, i think to myself,
will either be the most beautiful thing
to ever happen to me,
or the most ruinous.

perhaps though,
i wonder,
perhaps it could
somehow be
both.

god,
i'd let you
swallow me whole.
you're the only one
to ever make me
want to change
my plans.

—*revelation*

this is a eulogy
for the hatred i piled
onto my skin in recent years.

a funeral for all the doubt
i carried on my shoulders;
i am burying it now.

this is my apology
to the only body
i will ever have:

i am sorry for pinching you,
squeezing you into tight clothes,
crying over you,
telling you to be better
when you were already doing
all you could.

this is my promise
to do better.
to be forgiving.
to be kind.

you are doing
your very best.
it's time i do too.

i have become too complacent
with the feeling of wading through life,
half-submerged under waves
of obligations and requirements.

i'm coming up on land now,
gasping on freedom and
the way it feels in my lungs,
marveling at the sensation
of dry ground beneath my feet.

it's been a few months, and you finally feel like you can breathe again.

today when you woke up, your first thought was not about what happened to you. instead, it focused on the day ahead.

it didn't even occur to you to think of it at all until you were halfway through your morning. and when the first thought of it raced through your mind, you did not let it take hold. you didn't let it send you into a spiral. you thought it, you felt it, and your heart twinged for just a moment, but then . . . then it was over. it passed. and you kept moving.

throughout the day, that happened: small thoughts, bursts of memories. but each time, you let them wash over you, and then you carried on.

it was the best day you've had in a long time.

and tonight, you will fall asleep smiling.

the moon

you cling to
what has happened
to you because
you think it will
protect you.

and in some ways,
that is true—
it is good to remember
and to instill whatever
it might have taught you
deep inside.

but tell me,
must you hold it
so close to yourself?
does it really make
you feel safe,
or does it make you afraid
to ever believe in anything
true and good
again?

the night asks, who are you?
i answer,

well,
i am a musician
i am a daughter
i am a sister
i am a poet
i am a lover
i am a friend.

yes, but *who* are you?
i answer,

i think
i am a kind person
i am a worthy person
i am a good person
i am a smart person
i am a beautiful person.

do you *think*, or do you *know*?
and i say,

i know
i know
i know,

and i believe it.

i know
it can feel scary and hard
to shut out
the unreasonable expectations
and bitter judgment
that have become the soundtrack
to your existence.

but when you're sitting
in silence for the first time
in your whole life,
you will realize
just how worth it
it was.

—*mute button*

FOR YOUR CONSIDERATION:

what have you not yet
let go?
what part of your past
is still haunting you?

and how many more
times will you let it
ruin a chance at something
beautiful?

you were the first person
i felt both wildly unsure
and unwaveringly certain of.

that was the scariest part
about falling for you:
the fact that i had no idea
what i was doing,
but at the same time,
i knew exactly why
i had to.

—*once in a lifetime*

i remember that first night,
how i asked myself
if this is all you get,
will it be enough?

how ignorant i was
to think it ever
could have been.

i am ever growing,
ever changing.

if the last time
you saw me
was a month ago—
you might as well
get to know me
all over again.

i am not the same
as i was
last full moon.

i love you
in a way
that doesn't ever
let me stop
overthinking.

i am always one step ahead,
into the world where
i have already lost you.
and nobody else is in it.
just me.

when you yank me back,
i am surprised to find
you still standing there.
for a moment i don't know
what to do with your presence,
so i almost try to shake you off.

what i'm trying to say is,
when i feel like a lightning strike
and my voice sounds like a thunderstorm,
do not run from me.
let me rain. let me pour.
let me fall back into myself.

what i am trying to say is,
i know i am not always
the best to you.

but i am always trying
to be.

they don't talk enough about how hard it is to open yourself up again once something terrible has happened to you. because you've done the work. you've done the healing, and you're happy, so it should be easy, right? you should be holding your arms out in welcome.

but you're not. the thought of letting anybody in again is terrifying. their intentions all feel the same—ugly and slick—even if they aren't. you are afraid they will leave you suddenly, without warning. you are afraid they will rip open the grief you have so carefully sorted through and sealed away.

and with every new foot of distance you place between yourself and everyone else, you feel yourself growing lonelier. *was this the point,* you wonder, *was this the point of piecing myself back together, just to find myself unable to connect with anybody ever again, for fear of being back in that darkness?*

you don't know how to navigate this new terror, yet. but you know you will have to face it the same way you faced your trauma: slowly, with patience and understanding.

the sun

you have earned
this celebration.

every step of the way
has been leading
to this very moment.

so let your heart
flood with joy.

let it pour out of you.

let yourself
be surrounded by it.

in the mornings
i take my time.
i watch the way
the sunlight dapples
my skin through my curtains,
and i am grateful.

i am grateful for different things each day—
sometimes it is for the bright winter snow,
other times it is for my love, still asleep beside me,
or for the empty day i have ahead of me,
and sometimes it is simply
for the fact that i am
alive.

you are like a phoenix.

you rise from the ashes,
each time stronger
than the last.

just because
they did not see
the beauty they were holding
before they dropped you
does not mean
you are not beautiful.

some people
just don't realize
what they have
until after
they've let it go.

it's when i'm on the stage,
my soul pouring out of my body
in soaring melodies and outstretched arms,
when i look into the audience and see
the smiles or the tears or both,
when i feel the wave of applause
wash over me, that i think,

i may be unsure about so much,
but this is the one part of me
that will never falter.

i will always know
that this is where
i belong.

i look at you
sitting next to me,
and i wonder,

how long have i been stuck
in the dark,
waiting for a love like this
to come along and
light me up inside?

your fire doesn't always have to be

something that burns.

sometimes, your fire can be

something that warms,
something that lights,
something that helps.

use it as a weapon
when you must,
but that is not all it is.

you should never be afraid
of your natural spark.

—*when they call you feisty*

i don't know when our souls melded into one. maybe it was the moment we met. maybe it was the first time we kissed, or when we realized we loved each other. but you're my favorite part of every day. you're the best person i've ever met. i love you so much i don't even know what to do with it sometimes; i can't even put it into words. you're the reason i know it will always be okay. you are the future i can see so clearly now. you're the first person i share new things with. you're the only person i don't mind kissing with morning breath. i'd do it every morning for the rest of my life.

happiness is your constant companion now, and god, if it isn't the best feeling in the world. you are opening yourself to others again. you are letting yourself feel love for yourself and those around you. the feeling of stability and equilibrium you had and then so agonizingly lost has returned to you at last.

so today, you surround yourself with your friends. you drink and eat and laugh and smile. you tell them you love them, how grateful you are that they're in your life. and they tell you the same, all warm and bright and true.

you reflect on all you went through to get to this point. you won't ever understand why some of it happened—honestly, you don't believe it had to. but it did anyway, and you are here now, healed and rejuvenated and hopeful again.

it did not destroy you.

you think that even at your lowest, you always knew it wouldn't.

judgment

you can hear it now—
a soft cry,
beckoning you closer.

you have no doubt
that this is what
you have been waiting for.

so go on:

your purpose
is calling to you.

you must listen.

i say your name like a prayer,
my very own miracle
come to rest in
my two hands.

there will always be people trying to control you. there will always
be people snapping at your heels, trying to trip you up. you cannot
be liked by everyone. somebody will always find you too nice, too
mean, too much, too little, too big, too small, too this, too that.
but do you like what you see in the mirror? do you like the person
you have become and are continuing to grow into? do you sleep
at night smiling from another day well spent? there will always
be people who don't like you, but are they you? are they really the
ones that matter when it comes down to being who you are?

i started reading tarot on a random day in august, during the first year of the pandemic. i had been feeling lost and afraid; the state of the world was unclear, my love life was the least stable it had been in years, and i was entering my senior year of college and figuring out what, and where, i wanted my next step to be. i had heard from friends that tarot was something that grounded them, something that helped them feel less anxious in the face of so much uncertainty.

so i went to my local metaphysical shop and stared at the decks until i felt one call to me. i went home and did my first spread, googling the meanings and clumsily connecting the dots between each card. i don't remember exactly what that first spread said, but i do remember the first card i ever pulled: judgment, which speaks to renewal, awakening, and self-reflection. figuring out what it is you need to become your true self. making choices that will alter your life forever.

i didn't know what that meant, but i felt, even then, the weight of its truth: that i was on the cusp of something new, standing on the edge of the greatest period of transformation i had ever known.

—*august 2nd, 2020*

at the end
of my life,
i want to be able
to look back on
how i treated myself
and be proud of it.
i want to be able
to remember my 20s
and the relationship
i built with the world
with no regrets.

here's the thing
i've learned about
growing up:

it doesn't get easier,
you just get stronger.

you learn the lessons
and heal the wounds
and try to surround yourself
with the right people.

and then you hold on tight
and do your best
to enjoy the ride.

for the first time, i have found unconditional love. i did not know i'd yet to encounter it until it revealed itself to me. and when i felt it embrace me as i stared at you, it became obvious to me that everything had been lacking before you came along. to love free of conditions is life's greatest treasure. it is its most beautiful gift, and aren't i lucky to have found somebody who has helped me discover it. aren't we lucky to get to experience this together.

—*the joy of something new*

it's a time for reflection.

and as you look back, you feel nothing but pride. you are proud
of yourself. you took that small spark you felt all those months
ago, that urge to become something more, and you followed it,
nurtured it into the greatest flame, and now it burns within you,
bright and constant.

you remember how you hated yourself. how you let others control
you and hold you back. but no more of that. you are the one in
charge of your life. you can see that clearly now. it has always come
down to you and what it is you want for yourself, not anybody else.

so right now, you reflect.

and tomorrow, you live for you and you alone.

the world

what a wonder
it is
to finally feel
complete.

today is an unfolding of sorts.
i am waiting for the sun to rise.
waiting for the feeling of life on my skin,
for the signal that it is finally
time to bloom.

this is my secret:
i gave in to the urge. the urge to see everything around me as
beautiful. the urge to find joy in menial things and small moments.
i lined my windowsills with crystals, made a home out of the local
bookstore, found peace in the simplicity of ordering a coffee from
the same café each morning. i bathed myself in music. i lit candles
every day. i took photos and videos of the people i love so that i
would be able to have a memory of them forever.
but more than those things, i allowed myself to feel. i cried a lot.
i admitted things to myself that i would never have admitted a
year ago. i felt regret. i felt guilt. i felt anger. but i also felt gratitude
and hope and happiness. for the first time in my life, i tasted true
and utter contentment. over time, i began to feel, even in my
moments of grief or fury, that there was a sensation of something
i could only describe as *rightness* buzzing in the background. a
confirmation that this was the path i was meant to be on, that this
was the road i was destined to travel.
so i suppose what i am trying to tell you is that i did not come into
this way of living overnight. it was a long and often brutal process.
but when you know you're doing the right thing, you know. and i
knew.
do you?

today
i saw flowers blooming
in gardens and along the sidewalks,
marking the start of spring.

and the sun pressed
warm against my skin
like a soft kiss,
as though it were
an old lover coming back
home to me.

so often,
the small joys drift
through my fingers,
ghosts of something
long gone.

but today
i saw flowers blooming
in gardens and along sidewalks,
marking the start of spring,

and i did not let
the beauty of it
escape me.

i used to dream of a world
where he wouldn't scare me,
not in the slightest.
and for years,
i thought it impossible.

but here i am,
and it's almost funny
that he once was so large
and important.

i cannot wait for the day
when i walk into a room
and see him there,
and for the first time,
he will be the one who is

small.

—*he no longer matters*

i love you like air,
like fresh water,
like a necessity,
like kissing you is the same as breathing,
like everything i need to survive can be found
under your skin.

this is not a poem, but if it were, it would be the craziest one i've ever written. some nights i hold you so tightly it's like i'm afraid you will slip through my fingers. some nights i want to cry when i look at you, for good reasons. sometimes i think i love you so much it physically pains me, and i think maybe this will be what ruins me for the rest of my life. a lot of the time, i think that if you are not the one, it will be. i am going to spend a lifetime missing you if you are not by my side through it. i told myself i wouldn't let love do this to me again, but you are extremely persuasive. one time, you bit my thigh, and i swear i astral-projected. i've spent hours thinking about how my fingers feel inside your mouth. you tell me, *i just want to be skin-to-skin with you. i just want to feel close.* you hold me like i am breakable, and i suppose when it comes to you, i am. i'm a glass sculpture and you are the hammer and i am waiting, palms stretched wide, for the shattering blow. i can feel the cracks forming even now, and i admire them in the mirror, how they run along my fragile skin. i think this is the most beautiful i have ever been. this is me coming undone in your hands. i hear alarm bells in my head when i look at you, because every time our eyes meet i wonder if yours will be more hazel or green on our wedding day, and i have to stop myself, have to ask myself *what the fuck is wrong with you?* but then i think, *well, if it's a fall wedding, they'd probably look more green*, and i smile. i know i tell you all the time, but i think you're the most beautiful person ever created. i think we are all lucky to get to be alive at the same time as you, but i am definitely the luckiest because i'm the one you curl into at night. i'm the one who kisses you awake, who keeps your secrets, who sees the entirety of you. nobody else gets to be so lucky. anyway, i am glass and you are the hammer, or maybe we are both hammers. maybe we are both glass. i like that— us, equal even in breaking. what a spectacular collision we are. i think this is the most beautiful i have ever been: yours.

i wonder:
if the 16-year-old me could see me now,
what would she say?

if she could see the love i've found
compared to the love she had,

if she knew about all the dreams she carried
that i've watched come true,

would she smile?
would she cry?
would she say thank you?

or maybe i'd thank her.
thank her for her resilience
and her ambition.
thank her for her kindness
and her warmth.

i am who i am today
because of you, i'd say.
because you planted seeds
that i can now harvest.

and maybe she'd ask questions, like
what happened to him?
or where do you live?
all of which i'd answer truthfully.

and i'd watch her face fall
as i told her he wasn't the one,
then her smile return as i told her
about the person who was.

i'd wipe her tears as
she learned of all the times
things didn't quite work out,
and then see her celebrate
as she heard about all the times
things did.

there is a whole world
out there for us,
i'd tell her.

all we have to do
is reach for it.

you're sitting in the park in your neighborhood. it is sunny and warm. there is a slight breeze.

what is it that you want? that voice asked you all those months ago. you remember what you said. happiness. peace. beauty. how the voice told you you'd have to give it to yourself.

"and did you get what you wanted?" it asks now.

you look around. you see children playing in the playground, their laughter floating through the air. you see a couple on an afternoon stroll, their fingers intertwined and faces aglow with love. you hear the birds singing and the wind moving lazily through the trees.

and you see yourself, taking in the simplicity of it all, a fullness in your heart where once there was a gaping hole. you see yourself as you once were: small and scared, picking yourself apart each day, struggling to give yourself the love you've always deserved. the love you are now able to give freely. the light in you that once was so dim, come back at last.

"yes," you say softly, "i got it all, and then some."

the sun caresses your skin, and you feel content.

acknowledgments

there are many people that have had a part in the writing of this book, whether they're aware of it or not.

to michelle, i am glad to have found a publisher that is so dedicated to her authors and so understanding of my workload. (being an opera-singing poet in graduate school is not easy!) i am still very thankful that you decided to take a chance on me in 2020 and have continued to take chances on me since.

to my family, thank you for supporting me as i travel further into the world of adulthood, and for raising me the way you did. i am so grateful.

to alex, my most beloved: you are the best person i know. i cannot put into words how lucky i am to have met you and how much luckier i feel to get to love you and be loved in return. every day with you is the new best day of my life.

to ashley and kason, thank you for being such steadfast and reliant best friends. though we're no longer living in the same city (or in ashley's case, the same apartment), i know that we will always be there for each other.

to hunter, my creative soul mate, thank you for being such an avid supporter of my work, both musical and poetic. creating and singing with you has been some of the most fun i've ever had. i'm so glad we found each other, and i cannot wait to see what our unhinged brains create next.

to the poetry community, thank you for your support as i've grown up these last nine years. it has been a privilege and joy to come into adulthood as part of such a wonderful, warm community. i don't think i'll ever be able to repay you all enough for what you have given me.

to trista mateer, i have moments daily where i remember being in awe that you'd even like a post of mine. now, you are a trusted mentor and friend. i owe you so much. thank you.

to zane frederick, kaliane faye, and shelby leigh, thank you for all of your feedback on book ideas, listening to me rant about algorithms, and genuinely being some of the loveliest people i've ever met. i'm so excited to see where your talents will take you.

to jessica and molly, thank you for all the work you've done proofreading, editing, and improving this collection. you truly took this book to the next level. i'm so glad to have editors who are so considerate and diligent with their work.

to my teachers, past and present, i learned more from you than just the subject you taught in the classroom. i am who i am because of the wisdom and kindness you gave me. thank you.

and lastly, to my readers: thank you so much. this life i get to lead, sharing my poetry with all of you—it is surreal to me. i never thought it would be possible. but every day, i wake up and share poetry that, for whatever reason, touches your hearts, or helps to heal your wounds. thank you, thank you, thank you. i love you.

about the author

Catarine Hancock is a twenty-three-year-old poet and opera singer from Lexington, Kentucky. She holds a Bachelor of Music in Vocal Performance from the University of Kentucky, and is currently earning her Master of Music in Voice at Indiana University. Aside from music, poetry is her other great love. Having been a bookworm and writer all her life, she found her passion for poetry at the age of thirteen, and shortly afterward, she began sharing her writing online. Over the next nine years, her platform grew to an audience of over 300,000. She is the author of three other poetry collections, *shades of lovers* and *sometimes i fall asleep thinking about you,* and *sprout.* When she is not singing or writing, Catarine can be found curled up with a good fantasy novel, wandering the aisles of the local bookstore, or adding a weird décor item she found at Goodwill to her already too-cluttered apartment.

You can find Catarine here:
TikTok: @catarinehancock
Instagram: @catarinehancock
Twitter: @writingbych

about the illustrator

Divyani Jaiswal is a self-taught illustrator based in India. She is known on Instagram for her stunning visual art inspired by nature, songs, poetry, and movies.

You can learn more about or commission work from Divyani here:
Email: artofart2017@gmail.com
Instagram: @art_of_art___

discover more empowering poetry from central avenue

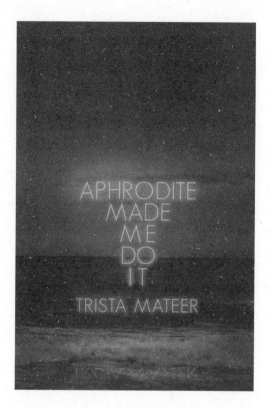

Bestselling and award-winning author Trista Mateer takes an imaginative approach to self-care in this poetry and prose collection, *Aphrodite Made Me Do It*. In this empowering retelling, she uses the mythology of the goddess to weave a common thread through the past and present. By the end of this book, Aphrodite will make you believe in the possibility of your own healing.

girl made of glass

shelby leigh

Girl Made of Glass is about how our past can
linger into our future. Broken into four parts,
this book is about finding, forgiving, and loving
ourselves. The Nightmares explores our past and
the moments that haunt us. The Mirror delves into
insecurity and how we might haunt ourselves. The
Shattering investigates relationships and how they
can break us. The Enchantment delivers an uplift-
ing conclusion of self-love and growth.